P9-BYZ-896

2.4

Z

SandCastle™

Baby
Australian Animals

It's a Baby
Kangaroo!

Kelly Doudna

Consulting Editor, Diane Craig, M.A./Reading Specialist

ABDO
Publishing Company

Published by ABDO Publishing Company, 8000 West 78th Street, Edina, Minnesota 55439.

Printed in the United States.

Editor: Liz Salzmann
Content Developer: Nancy Tuminelly
Cover and Interior Design and Production: Kelly Doudna, Mighty Media
Photo Credits: iStockphoto (LeeTorrens), Peter Arnold Inc. (John Cancalosi, Gunter Ziesler), Shutterstock

Library of Congress Cataloging-in-Publication Data

Doudna, Kelly, 1963-
  It's a baby kangaroo! / Kelly Doudna.
     p. cm. -- (Baby Australian animals)
  ISBN 978-1-60453-576-1
  1. Kangaroos--Infancy--Juvenile literature. I. Title.

  QL737.M35D68 2010
  599.2'22139--dc22
                          2008055075

SandCastle™ Level: Fluent

SandCastle™ books are created by a team of professional educators, reading specialists, and content developers around five essential components—phonemic awareness, phonics, vocabulary, text comprehension, and fluency—to assist young readers as they develop reading skills and strategies and increase their general knowledge. All books are written, reviewed, and leveled for guided reading, early reading intervention, and Accelerated Reader® programs for use in shared, guided, and independent reading and writing activities to support a balanced approach to literacy instruction. The SandCastle™ series has four levels that correspond to early literacy development. The levels are provided to help teachers and parents select appropriate books for young readers.

| **Emerging Readers** | **Beginning Readers** | **Transitional Readers** | **Fluent Readers** |
| (no flags) | (1 flag) | (2 flags) | (3 flags) |

SandCastle™ would like to hear from you. Please send us your comments and suggestions.
sandcastle@abdopublishing.com

Vital Statistics

for the Kangaroo

BABY NAME
joey

NUMBER IN LITTER
1

WEIGHT AT BIRTH
$\frac{3}{100}$ ounce (less than 1 g)

AGE OF INDEPENDENCE
12 to 18 months

ADULT WEIGHT
70 to 200 pounds (32 to 90 kg)

LIFE EXPECTANCY
7 to 10 years

Kangaroos are **marsupials**.
A baby kangaroo is called
a joey.

A **female** usually has one
joey at a time.

5

A joey stays in its mother's pouch for about eight months. Then it begins going for short hops outside the pouch.

A joey continues to **nurse** even after it leaves its mother's pouch.

Kangaroos are **herbivores**.
They live on open plains
and eat the long grasses
that grow there.

Kangaroos usually eat at
night when it is cool.

9

Kangaroos live in groups called mobs. A mob includes a strong **male** and several **females** and their joeys.

There are usually about ten kangaroos in a mob.

11

Kangaroos **communicate** with clucks and coughs. They stomp their back feet to warn other kangaroos of danger.

The **dingo** is the only animal that **preys** on kangaroos. Other dangers are hunters and being hit by cars.

Kangaroos hop as their main way of moving around. Their large back feet make it hard for them to walk.

Kangaroos can hop as fast as 35 miles per hour (56 km/h).

The tail of a kangaroo is very strong. A kangaroo can **balance** its full weight on its tail. Then it can use all four feet to fight.

Kangaroo fighting is called boxing. It looks like they are **punching** each other.

19

A joey becomes **independent** when its mother won't let it **nurse** anymore.

Fun Fact

About the Kangaroo

An adult kangaroo can leap 30 feet (9 m) at a time. That's as long as a fire truck!

30 feet (9 m)

Glossary

balance – to keep level without tipping to one side or the other.

communicate – to share ideas, information, or feelings.

dingo – an Australian wild dog.

female – being of the sex that can produce eggs or give birth. Mothers are female.

herbivore – an animal that eats only plants.

independent – not relying on others for care or support.

male – being of the sex that can father offspring. Fathers are male.

marsupial – a mammal in which the female has a pouch in which the young develop.

nurse – to drink milk from a mother's breast.

prey – to hunt or catch an animal for food.

punch – to hit with a closed fist.

To see a complete list of SandCastle™ books and other nonfiction titles from ABDO Publishing Company, visit **www.abdopublishing.com**.

8000 West 78th Street, Edina, MN 55439

800-800-1312 • 952-831-1632 fax